the garden and the graveyard

the GARden and the GRAVeyARd

Sermons on Genesis for Lent and Easter

by George M. Bass

AUGSBURG PUBLISHING HOUSE
Minneapolis   Minnesota

THE GARDEN AND THE GRAVEYARD

Library of Congress Catalog Card No. 71-135214

International Standard Book No. 0-8066-1101-4

Manufactured in the United States of America

To George Jr., and Donna
my son and daughter

that there might be a garden
for them and their loved ones
to live in.

Contents

the fate and the future of lent

The Fate and the Future of Lent

A congregation in central Pennsylvania has reduced
Lent to its original two-week period. A church in Cali-
fornia has eliminated Lent altogether. Another parish
has replaced special worship services with discussion
groups that consider the problems of contemporary
life. Many pastors in the Roman Catholic and Lutheran
stronghold in Minnesota have substituted chancel dra-
mas for preaching and prayer services during Lent.
The facts indicate that Lent is not what it used to be
in the life of the church. It is time to ask questions
like these:

1. Should Lent be taken seriously any longer, and does
it have sufficient value for the contemporary church to
warrant its retention and reformation?

2. If Lent still has some value, should preaching be em-
phasized as it has been in the past?

These and similar questions ought to be asked and
answered in the light of the dilemma that Lent is in
today.

The Self-Evident Problems in Lent

For more than a decade church leaders and preachers have been saying that Lent is an anachronism. They say Lent is too long. In a fast moving world spiritual attention and momentum lag over a six and one-half week penitential season; by the middle of Lent interest and attendance at special and even regular Sunday services lag noticeably. A corresponding diminution in personal and family devotional activities follows naturally.

Another, and perhaps more serious charge is that the Lenten themes sounded by preachers are not pertinent to the needs of the world today. Lent proclaims something that happened two thousand years ago. The suffering and death of one man in the distant past doesn't seem to say much to a world in which cruelty, terror, and murder abound, where napalm roasts the innocent as well as the military, where hunger and famine are becoming commonplace, and disaster may go almost unnoticed. The contemporary "peace symbol" seems to have more pertinence than the cross of Christ and the gospel. Lent is an outmoded liturgical and devotional exercise, it would appear, to countless church members today.

An increasingly large number of critics fault the church for proliferating preaching during Lent as a kind of futile gesture of defiance toward the multimedia age of communication. The truth is that in Protestantism, at least, Lent is celebrated primarily through preaching, and preaching, according to some communication experts, needs to be de-emphasized, or even replaced by new media for the communication of a contemporary message to church and world.

Some Deeper Issues

There is enough truth in most of the charges being made about Lent to demand a closer look at the deeper issues involved in the dilemma of Lent. Such a study leads to the following conclusions:

1. The nature of Lent is not really understood by the church—people or preachers. Lent is seen as a season that deals with the death of Christ; while it really delineates the death of every man who ever lived.

2. Since more often than not, the celebration of Lent begins at the cross, Lent is a kind of circular season that ends where it began. It should be a time of going up, a journey to the cross and tomb.

3. Lent is not simply devotional; it is sacramental. The faithful should proceed to the front, where they "die" and "rise" with Christ, and to the table where the risen Lord is the host.

4. The structure of the season is usually ignored, particularly during the problem period, the first four and one-half weeks of Lent. Since structure selects the themes of worship and preaching, thematic problems result. The sin of man is treated too generally, or strictly as a biblical phenomenon connected with the crucifixion of Christ, without the nature and consequences of sin right now, being spelled out.

5. Lent is not overemphasized; it is misemphasized so that Lent dominates Easter, reducing it to a one-day celebration. In this process the gospel suffers a terrible fate; it loses its thrust toward new life in Christ.

If Lent is to escape the fate threatening it and have any future at all, the preachers of the church will have to take a fresh look at the season before they plan their worship celebrations and pick their sermon themes. To do anything less than this may relegate Lent to total oblivion.

The Legacy of Lent

Lent is meant to be a time of involvement for the entire Christian community. Lent concerns every person of every parish, because Lent is concerned with man's common and continuing curse, death. Death knows no spectators; every person is a participant in the struggle to understand and overcome this hated enemy. When God said to Adam and Eve, "You are dust, and to dust you shall return," the whole race was included. No one has escaped this specter since that terrible day. Lent has been, and still must be, a time when people face up to death and its cause, sin.

Lent helps people to understand that sin was not only responsible for Jesus' death, for it made the cross necessary, but that sin destroys every man. Lent paints the picture of man's wilful pride and rebellion in such a way that people may come to understand and confess their rebellion against God.

But Lent always and ultimately confronts the Christian community with a God who loves his creatures so much that he never gives up on them. A word from the past etches the cross, on the problems and crises of the present in order to cause man to pause and ponder the magnificence of this mystery. That cross demonstrates for all time and all men the lengths to which God will go to save his creatures from themselves.

Lent, therefore, is a time when the church remembers that God has an ultimate purpose for the human race. What he intends transcends time and space; the Scriptures show that his purpose concerns eternity and another "world" hidden from the view of man. How awful it would be if God had created man in his image, given him the ability to discern his destiny, and then left him to his deserved fate—destruction and death. "Let not your hearts be troubled," said our Lord. "The last enemy to be destroyed is death," added Paul.

Lent is a period when the wisdom and power of God are pitted against the problems that man has created, the difficulties that threaten all life with destruction. It is the occasion when the church should probe for the causes that challenge the continued existence of life on earth. The probing has to be done in the heart of man, because most of man's problems have a spiritual source. An ecologist commented on the total predicament of mankind today as he told a group of conservationists how beautiful Lake Minnetonka, just west of Minneapolis, could be saved from the peril of pollution: "The lake can be saved if some people will move away from its shoreline. The trouble is that no one wants to move. The real problem, therefore, is in the heart of man, and that's why I can't be very optimistic about the preservation of this lake." Lent opens up the human heart with God's sharp scalpel, the Word and the Spirit, and seeks to repair the damage. Lent offers drastic surgery, not simply an exploratory operation, so that man might survive.

Ultimately, the legacy of Lent offers hope to humanity through the gospel of our Lord, the personal action God took to rescue man from sin and death, and in the process to reveal a kind of "return to paradise." The cross and tomb are strong, stark symbols of God's existence, love, concern, and power massed in Christ against the destructive forces at work in the world. It inspires the sort of prayer James S. Stewart once offered at the beginning of a class in preaching: "Grant that we may not be so obsessed with the chaos of this world that we lose the sense of Jesus' majesty, nor that we be so overwhelmed by its problems that we lose the exhilaration of the gospel. . . ."

Lent gives man a way of looking at the world, himself, and God, through the gospel, that kindles hope for the whole race. Sin and separation, death and destruction, have been defeated once and for all, and man has nothing to fear.

Investing the Legacy of Lent

Lent is like a match struck in the darkness of midnight; its light burns brightly and quickly goes out, swallowed up by the darkness it sought to overcome. The legacy of Lent, passed down to our day, does light up the darkness, but it stands in jeopardy of dying out so that it will be lost forever. To keep Lent burning brightly, its legacy must be recognized and invested in our lives, or it will be lost forever.

This means that Lent must be thematically linked to Easter as it runs its annual six and one-half week course, and the connection should continue and develop in the seven week Easter season. As it is now celebrated, Lent virtually eliminates Eastertide; Lent is a 40-day season, while Easter is reduced to a one-day seasonal remnant. To correct this overemphasis, the "little Easter" note of Christ's resurrection and reign must be imprinted on the entire Lenten season. The perspective of Lent is the empty tomb, as well as the cross of Calvary, and a subdued "Christ is risen! Alleluia!" is sounded with a proper celebration of each Sunday in Lent. Unless the note of victory and triumph permeates the whole period, Lent is an operation in futility. Despite popular opinion and practice, Lent is not more important than Easter. To be of contemporary value to the church, this perspective needs to be reestablished as it is found in the gospel.

Before the full and true legacy of Lent can be invested again in the church and contemporary society, the preachers of the church must recognize the forgotten, but thematically indispensable, structure of the season. The structure has built-in themes for each part of Lent so that there is a progression of themes from Ash Wednesday to Easter Sunday. Contrary to common practice and preaching, Lent does not deal with the passion and death of Christ for six and one-half weeks. These are the themes for the last two weeks of Lent, Passiontide. By concentrating concern for Christ and his cross in this latter period, the preacher liberates the rest of the season and makes possible the beneficial investment of the full legacy of Lent.

The first four and one-half weeks of Lent deal with the predicament of man, not the cross and death of Christ. Although the gospel on Quinquagesima Sunday declares, "Behold, we are going up to Jerusalem, and everything that is written of the Son of man by the prophets will be accomplished . . .; they will scourge and kill him. . . ." (Luke 18:31, 33), Ash Wednesday's theme says nothing about the crucifixion; it speaks to man in *his* predicament. The underlying theme of Ash Wednesday and the first four and one-half weeks of Lent comes from Genesis 3:19b, ". . . you are dust, and to dust you shall return," and the gospel points men to the kingdom of heaven, "Do not lay up for yourselves treasures on earth, where moth and rust consume and where thieves break in and steal, but lay up for yourselves treasures in heaven. . . . For where your treasure is, there will your heart be also"

(Matthew 6:19-21). This period should speak to all of the perplexities that man encounters in life before the call to cross and tomb goes out in the last two weeks of Lent. The cross is meant for a dying world as a divine hand extended to drowning humanity, and people eagerly grasp and cling to it when they see their predicament.

Understanding the structure of the season encourages the preacher to differentiate between the predicament of man and the passion of Christ. By the inclusion of a biblical perspective, he is able to show that the cross means reconciliation and re-creation for the people who participate in the pilgrimage. He will show that Lent is kept for Easter, as well as Good Friday, for when Lent exists for its own sake its legacy is largely lost.

It becomes rather obvious that contemporary preaching in Lent calls for new themes, as well as some new ways to communicate these themes. They must be contemporary, if they are to have any value and importance. They must confront the issues of life and death—population explosion, people pressure, pollution, production and distribution of food, war and murder, crime and punishment, birth control and abortion—and always in the light of the redemptive and saving action of God at cross *and* tomb.

Any new themes used in the worship and preaching of Lent may be reinforced and complemented by other media such as drama, film, and discussion. The church will have to use every means at her disposal to present the claims of Christ and the promises of the gospel to a world in conflict and crisis. But the church must not forget the uniqueness of preaching in the process; rather, the church must seek to improve the message and delivery of the sermon. New forms and, even more, new language are needed for the upgrading of the sermon. And finally, worship will have to undergo the same kinds of radical treatment at work in the contemporary world if the full value of Lent is to be recovered.

One more suggestion: the church can rediscover and make profitable use of the pre-Lenten Sundays, a period when the church can ready for Lent by making posters, erecting banners, planning special programs and activities which have to do with Lent and contemporary "Christ and Crisis" themes. This is the time when the church needs to be called together, informed about the destination and purpose of the Lenten pilgrimage, chart the course as a community, and begin the march that holds the temporal and eternal destiny of man in the balance.

A Perspective for Pertinent Preaching

Septuagesima Sunday once marked the beginning of the Christian year and the church began to read the Bible *lectio continua* fashion in daily worship and devotions. This reading began with the first book of the

Bible, Genesis. Contemporary needs and usages suggest that the church might supplement the traditional pericopes with the reading of Genesis, starting with Ash Wednesday. Selected passages and themes might be used at worship during the week to complement the Sunday topics.

Genesis is disturbingly relevant to man's situation and the ecological-environmental crisis of our world. From the perspective of the creation of the world, God addresses man in his predicament. He speaks to his sinful waste and the "loss of paradise," to his greed and disobedience in the light of his Genesis admonitions to man to "take dominion over the earth" and life—manage it wisely—and to "populate the earth" and "fill it up."

Genesis shows the punishment that is not merely decreed by God upon those who disobey his Word, but is built into his creation. Disobedience leads to destruction and death, not only in every age and for every man, but also as a general and ultimate judgment upon the children of Adam. Man has always wanted to be God, or at least to control God, rather than to fulfill his destiny—to worship and serve his God.

The book of Genesis is alarmingly appropriate to a world that thought it had disposed of God and was getting along quite nicely without him. Every time man thinks he is independent of God, he discovers how much he needs God's help. Every time man

thinks he has it "made," suddenly he discovers that he
has only been digging his own grave.

At the same time, Genesis reveals the love and
patience of God—"I will not destroy man with a flood"
—in such a way as to indicate the promise of the gospel. He will always help his children, if only they will
hear and heed him. He offers rescue from sin and
death, the power of his spirit to counterbalance the
influence of evil, and the mysterious power of the
Word that can make a new creation out of sinful man.

By reading and preaching on the texts and themes
from Genesis for the first four and one-half weeks of
Lent, Ash Wednesday to Passion Sunday, the perceptive pastor can proclaim the gospel powerfully and
pertinently to a world in which men perceive that time
is running out on them. "The heart of man is laid
bare" during this time. During the last two weeks, "the
heart of God is laid bare" and offered to mankind
through the gracious sacrifice and death of Jesus Christ.
The age-old threat of Genesis, "You are dust, and to
dust you shall return," is countered by the cross of
Christ. Through Genesis and the gospel God offers
hope to a world committing genocide.

Lent has value for a world in crisis. Since it is concerned with man's relationship with God, with his
spiritual condition as it relates to the condition and
crisis in the world, and the new possibilities for mankind in Christ and the gospel, Lent needs to be re-
tained. It follows that preaching, overhauled and re-

conditioned in theme and form, is also an imperative for the contemporary church. Informed by Genesis and the gospel, such preaching might make the difference between the life and death of the whole human race.

SERMONS ON GENESIS

1.

Genesis 3:17a, 19:

And to Adam he said, . . . "In the sweat of your face you shall eat bread till you return to the ground, for out of it you were taken; you are dust, and to dust you shall return."

A Garden and
a Graveyard

Lent begins on an eternally disturbing note—death!
Everyone knows that Lent has to do with the suffering and death of Jesus Christ. It is a penitential period that may be entered with prayer and objective devotion:

> Sweet the moments, rich in blessing,
> Which before the Cross we spend;
> Life and health and peace possessing
> From the sinner's dying Friend.
> *(SBH* 63, stanza 1)

Lent is a lengthy journey to Calvary, where the faithful remember and meditate on the death of Jesus Christ.

But Lent contains a surprise for the people who undertake this seemingly harmless religious pilgrimage; they are confronted by their own threatened death, not Christ's. A word from the dim, distant past makes a discordant sound as Lent begins: "Man, you are dust, and unto dust you shall return."

The destination for Lenten pilgrims is an open grave, not simply a cross over a cave outside Jerusalem. A Roman Catholic congregation in Wisconsin understands this. One Good Friday the pastor of this parish startled his congregation by placing an open casket before the altar. When the Good Friday service was concluded, he directed the people to file past the bier and peer into that open casket. Each person found himself looking into his own casket; he could see only himself in the casket, because it was lined with a mirror that silently uttered the same sentence of death to each viewer, "You are dust, and to dust you shall return." It was a shocking experience for those who went to the coffin. Many, for the first time in their lives, really learned that Lent is about the death of every man, as well as the death of Christ.

Death is always outrageous. It always awakens bitterness and resentment in the human heart when it intrudes on life and the living. Helmut Thielicke in *How the World Began* could be speaking for every thinking man when he writes:

> Why should death exist? Why should the fate of men be like that of the beasts (cf. Eccles. 3:19)? Why cannot even the strongest love hold on to another when his hour has come? Why is the birth of new life accompanied by pain and dread and peril of death? Why do thorns and thistles encumber the fields? Why does frost fall upon the springtime blossom? Why should we be at enmity with nature,

which, after all, was once the Garden of Eden? Why should the horror of infantile paralysis exist alongside the miracle of new life?

Always, always the question: Why? Why? The awful thing about being a man is in having the ability to perceive the dimensions of mortality and the knowledge of death. Man has always asked, Why? Why do *I* have to die? Quickly, another question is posed, "Isn't there some way out of this predicament, death, that confronts me?"

Ever since the garden experience with God, men have been trying to overcome or circumvent death. As they speak of a "fountain of youth," a Shangri-La type of paradise, or simply of conquering disease and death, it is apparent that they are groping for the garden of life again. The shroud of death hangs before the face of all mankind. But that shroud cannot be ripped open, from the bottom upwards, by mere mortals. God alone, who hung it there, can rend it. And this he did in Christ through the cross and the cave-tomb that couldn't hold him.

With typical sophistication modern man has pinned his hopes to conquer death on science and the "open sesame" of space. Until recently, more than a few people have believed that time could be overcome in the far reaches of the universe. Perhaps other planets could be colonized and the problems of earth, including death, might be banished by a breed of bold and brainy adventurers that break out of the bonds of life on earth.

Thousands of years after the legendary Odysseus heard a goddess singing on an enchanted isle, luring him and his men to a place where the sailors were turned into pigs, a siren song sounded from deep space to modern man, offering hope and the promise of paradise. But it appears as if earth is really the only place the human race has in which to live. Lord C. P. Snow in an article in *Look* (August 26, 1969) interpreted the meaning of man's first successful landing on another heavenly body, the moon, this way:

> We desperately need something to take us out—not constantly but part of the time, out of this our mundane life. For generations the hope of heaven did this, as long as people could believe that heaven was up there, somewhere beyond the sky. It was a naive idea, but very powerful. And nothing more sophisticated has ever become more powerful. . . . We know now that the only lives we shall ever meet turn out to be our own.

Heaven itself and eternal life as well, have retreated before the 20th century space probes. Man is still mortal, and he has to live on the earth—and die there, too.

"Man, you are dust."

The uniqueness of the latter part of the 20th century is that, for the first time in the history of humanity, it is possible scientifically to predict the extinction of all people, perhaps all life, on the earth. Alexander Coxe sang of the contradictions of an age when people could say with understanding, "in the midst of life we are in death."

> We are living, we are dwelling, in a grand and awful time.
> In an age on ages telling to be living is sublime.
> Hark! the waking up of nations; Gog and Magog to the fray.
> Hark! what soundeth? 'Tis creation groaning for its latter day.

Man has been living in a graveyard all the time. Suddenly, everyone knows it!

"Earth to earth, ashes to ashes, dust to dust. . . ."

Man's excesses have caught up with him—polluted air and water, crumbling cities and cluttered countrysides, impending famine, the constant specter of war and hatred and the generation-old "bomb," all coupled with the materialistic myth, "it is ours to do with what we will." Surely, the garden hasn't been regained. Paradise is still lost! The muffled drum beats time for man's funeral march!

"To dust . . . . to dust . . . . to dust . . ."

Without Lent man would go mad. Lent offers hope to dying men and to a race about to become extinct. It says "In the midst of death, we are in life!" God anticipated man's mismanagement of the earth and his misuse of the freedom with which he endowed mankind at the beginning, and so God stepped into the world, the graveyard, in Jesus Christ. He came offering life to all who hear and answer his invitation, "Come unto me, all of you. . ." The offer is good for time and eternity, for the conquest of sin and death and for the preservation of humanity.

The "catch" is just this: to receive God's gift in Christ, life, it is necessary to die, spiritually and right now. That is what Lent is all about—our death as well as Christ's, our death *in* the Lord, so that as we die in him we might be born to new life and live in him as well.

Lent is not simply about the cross of Christ; it is about the open grave in front of mankind, which Jesus dared to enter so long ago. Lent is about the font, wherein we enter into the waters of death and come forth as new beings. And our Lord has prepared a table before us, spreading out a banquet of new life, for the graveyard is a garden again.

As you enter the main-side door of Northwestern Lutheran Seminary chapel in St. Paul for the first time, your eyes meet a shocking sight. Right in front of you is Paul Theodore Granlund's "Christ Figure," a contemporary crucifix made of ladder-scaffolding twisted together to hold up pieces of planks that form the crossbar from which the corpus hangs in death. The dead Christ confronts everyone who enters the chapel. Just as you see the body and face of the one who said, "And I, if I be lifted up, will draw all men unto myself," you discover you are right beside the baptismal font—and suddenly you know why the "Christ Figure" is located where it is and faces the door on the side as it does: "Do you not know that all of us who have been baptized into Christ Jesus were baptized into his death? We were buried therefore with him by baptism into death, so that as Christ was raised from the dead by the glory of the Father, we too might walk in newness of life."

Lent is about death, but it is about life—ours, yours, mine, the life of the whole human race. It spells out a death sentence—"to dust you shall return"—in the graveyard, Earth. But through the cross that was plunged into the earth, a wedge was driven into the common grave of humanity, so that man might get back to the garden—and life—once more.

2.

Genesis 1:26-31:

"Let us make man in our image, after our likeness. . . . Be fruitful and multiply, and fill the earth and subdue it; and have dominion . . ." And God saw everything that he had made, and behold, it was very good.

God's Gamble in
the Garden

Some say St. Francis said it:

> The kiss of the sun for pardon;
> The song of the birds for mirth;
> One is nearer God's heart in a garden
> Than anywhere else on earth.

That has been true since the beginning of it all, the creation.

The process of creation ultimately resulted in the production of a garden. The earth was a paradise, much like an oasis in the desert. It was perfect in every detail when man first came on the scene. It had to be. Conditions had to be just right for the production and sustenance of mankind. When garden-like conditions existed on the earth, man appeared in the garden that God had prepared.

In a sense, God has no one but himself to blame for what has happened to the garden since the creation of man. God gave the garden to man to manage, to use, to populate—with virtually no strings attached. God gave only two commands to mankind: (1) take dominion, subdue, and manage the earth; and (2) fill it up. That's all man needed; he began to take charge of things right away!

But apparently man misunderstood. He quickly discovered that he could dominate and domesticate most other forms of animal life. What he couldn't tame, he tried to eliminate. Wild and domestic life of all forms bent before his will and purposes.

The late-comer became a looter. He found the earth more difficult to subdue and control than the forms of life on it. Nature has always proved to be too much for man. To this day he exerts little control over it; he is able to predict the weather to a remarkable degree, but he can never guarantee what will happen. His best efforts have been in protecting himself from the power of the elements which nature unleashes from time to time. Perhaps it is because of this that he seems to try to retaliate by using the earth and its resources as if they were totally his rather than a trust from God.

Robert Louis Stevenson could have been the first man in the garden, discovering the riches and resources of earth with newly opened eyes, when he wrote: "The world is so full of a number of things, I'm sure we should all be as happy as kings." They are the words of a nearly contemporary man who discovered a kind of paradise in the South Seas. He only spoke of what Adam saw and set out to enjoy. God took a chance when he opened his treasures and set them out before man. He had no doubts but that man would delight in them, but he must have had misgivings about the way people would use them.

A suburban high school outside of Minneapolis-St. Paul gathered and reconditioned toys for poor children as a Christmas project. Everything they collected was in, or put in, virtually new condition, and then the toys were given to churches and social agencies for distribution in the inner city. The news media through camera and video tape went with a black pastor as he distributed toys in the neighborhood where his church was located. He took a bicycle into the home of a young boy, and he selected a doll for the boy's sister. The boy was delighted at his gift, but the little girl was the picture of unrestrained joy. Her face lit up as soon as she saw her doll. She couldn't stand still; she began to jump up and down in pure ecstasy. She had received her heart's desire, a wondrous gift, and could not contain herself. And here is a picture of man's reaction to the wonders of the earth; at least, it shows what man's joy ought to be in the light of God's gracious gifts on earth.

The real question is not whether the child was grateful for the doll at the moment she received it, but whether or not she cared for it with the same spirit she expressed when she received it. The donors, in a much lesser way, took the same kind of gamble God took in the garden when they gave the child that doll.

I wonder what it looked like six months after she jumped with joy when it was placed in her arms at Christmas.

We know what the earth looks like. Anyone can see what has been happening since the beginning of time. The remains of mines whose value has been depleted, and the ghost towns left by the ruins. The stark skeletons of cities set on hills and castles built as men tried to reach for the sky. Great pits gouged out of the ground; holes flooded with so much water that they cannot be pumped out; shafts and tunnels in which fires perpetually burn—virtual hell-holes. Trees torn up, and fields that are washed away by the rains. Streams, once pure, that will not even sustain the roughest fish. And the cities which so eloquently speak of man's lack of care and concern for earth and the life of his fellow creatures.

With regularity and dramatic consequences the earth strikes back. She attempts to wash herself with flash floods, to blow away the polluters with hurricane and tornado. Now and again, she opens her mouth, through earthquake or man-made disaster, and attempts to swallow up as much of the human race as possible.

How well I remember a mine cave in northeastern Pennsylvania when I was just starting school. Most of the city in which we lived was honey-combed with mine shafts and tunnels. Mine caves were quite common, for "played out" mines were never filled in. One morning a few bricks were missing between the trolley tracks very near to our home. By noon half of the street had disappeared, and by evening there was a cave that stretched almost from curb to curb. Since the cave-in occurred during the daylight hours, no one was injured or killed. Had it happened at night, or in some one's basement or backyard, quite common occurrences, who knows what the results would have been.

God seems to be losing the gamble he took with man in the garden. But he hasn't lost it yet. It is almost as if the dice were still rolling—some of the earth-plunderers are beginning to see their folly. Some men are becoming responsible and are taking their earth-keeping tasks quite seriously. A builder buys a small farm with a slimy, treeless, pond on it. The little lake was a miniature edition of other polluted bodies of water, beyond any hope of usefulness. But the builder had foresight; he cleaned the banks, planted grass, shrubs, and trees, dredged out the muck and debris that had accumulated for years, and the pond was rejuvenated. Before he built any houses in the area, he put up a sign, Winchester Pond.

In small projects like that men are beginning to practice conservation in the way that God intended when he made the garden; the garden wall is being repaired, and the plans for the garden are being re-studied. A word from the writer of Proverbs is heard round the world. "Where there is no vision, the people perish." And perceptive people realize that the restoration of a vision of God, the earth as his garden, and his intentions for mankind on the earth is the most perplexing problem to be faced.

Could it be that only the cross of Christ can restore such vision to men? Can it be that from the cross alone man can see the garden as it was in the beginning and as God intends it to be made new again? Christ came to make all things new. And what he sets out to do he accomplishes in God's good time!

3.

Genesis 4:1-16, especially vv. 9-11:

Then the Lord said to Cain, "Where is Abel your brother?" He said, "I do not know; am I my brother's keeper?" And the Lord said, "What have you done? The voice of your brother's blood is crying to me from the ground. And now you are cursed from the ground, which has opened its mouth to receive your brother's blood from your hand."

The Ultimate
Madness

Life is God's greatest gift to the world and man is the highest form of expression of that gift. Created in the image of God, man is to be viewed with wonder and awe, for the life of man is precious. God alone can give and create it. Life is precious, sacred, and mysterious.

That's what Ray Bradbury was trying to say to the world after the first atom bombs had been dropped on Hiroshima and Nagasaki, as it became apparent that the bomb would hang over the heads of men for years to come, threatening the world with a holocaust that would consume all life. He pictured an imaginary incident on Mars toward the end of the first quarter of the 21st century. A spaceship from earth, which has been on a 20 year exploratory trip into deep space, returns to Mars to pick up a Mr. Hathaway, an ingenious scientist, and his family and take them back to earth. A joyous reunion occurs between Hathaway and Captain Wilder and his lieutenant, Williamson;

the men make plans to return to earth. As they enjoy a festive breakfast, Williamson discovers that something is wrong with Hathaway's family; his wife and children look exactly as they did two decades before. Suspicious, Williamson conducts a search and discovers four graves. Hathaway's wife and children have been dead for years. Somehow or other, Hathaway has created robot replacements for his family who are not only life-like in their perfection, but ageless, too.

The excitement of the reunion proves too much for Hathaway. He has a heart attack and dies. His death precipitates a dilemma for Wilder and his crew, articulated by Williamson: "What are we going to do about them?"

"I don't know," said the captain.

"Are you going to turn them off?"

"Off?" The captain looked faintly surprised. "It never entered my mind."

"You're not going to take them back with us?"

"No, it would be useless."

"You mean you're going to leave them here, like *that,* as they *are!*"

The captain handed Williamson a gun. "If you can do anything about this, you're a better man than I."

Five minutes later Williamson returned. "Here, take your gun. I understand what you mean now. I went in the hut with the gun. One of the daughters smiled at me. So did the others. The wife offered me a cup of tea. Lord, it'd be murder."

Wilder nodded. "There'll never be anything as fine as them again. They're built to last; ten, fifty, two hundred years. Yes, they've as much right to—to life as you or I or any of us." He knocked out his pipe. "Well, get aboard. We're taking off. . . ." And after an uncontrollable impulse sent Williamson back to say goodby to the "family," they did just that.

Man's ultimate madness is his lack of appreciation for life on earth, especially for the life of his own kind. His real "impossible dream" involves an appreciation for life that is expressed by holding people in high regard and loving his fellowman in positive ways. He doesn't seem able to see life from God's perspective, as the poet did:

> Dreams are they, but they are God's dreams. Shall we decry or scorn them?
> That men shall love one another; That white shall call black man brother;
> That greed shall pass from the market place; That lust shall yield to love for the race;
> That man shall meet with God, face to face;
> Dreams are they all, but shall we despise them, God's dreams?
> Dreams are they, to become man's dreams. Shall we say "nay" as they claim us?
> That men shall cease from their hating; That war shall soon be abating;
> That the glory of kings and lords shall pale; That the pride of power and dominion shall fail;
> That the love of humanity shall prevail.

Dreams are they all, but shall we despise them, God's
dreams?

What Cain started out in a field outside the garden
has continued and been expanded. If anything, man
has refined his methods of showing disdain for his
fellowman and for the precious life with which God
has endowed mankind. Regardless of war or peace,
the onslaught continues. Man plunders and persecutes
and maims and kills, and the mouth of the earth opens
wide to receive the life God gave.

Man never learns. Visit the ancient and holy city of
Jerusalem and it is possible to see this truth demon-
strated in dramatic fashion. Go to a low and striking
temporary building in the "new" city and see a ceremony that takes place every morning at 11 o'clock.
People pack the perimeter of the place, standing be-
hind fence-like railings on two sides of the room. In
one corner, inside the barriers, several people stand on
a low platform. Between them and the others is a large
expanse of floor. It has 20 names imprinted on it in
very legible letters: Auschwitz, Dachau, Belsen, Buch-
enwald. . . All of the infamous Nazi concentration
camps, with their gas chambers, ovens, and mass graves
plowed into the ground are there. With the speeches
of remembrance for the lives of the more than 6 million Jews exterminated in Europe during World War
II, the beautifully chanted and haunting prayers, and
the relighting of the "eternal flame" to their memory,

emotion is everywhere evident. Not many, young or old, who watch this daily ceremony, have dry eyes. And yet, it seems to do little to change their regard for the lives of their fellowmen, even for the Arabs living in Palestine. Their refugee camps seem almost to be concentration camps; their lot so difficult that one almost wonders if death might not be preferable. One must ask, "How long, Lord? How long?" After all, this is but a vignette of the larger, world-wide situation brought about by man's disdain for any life but his own.

Modern man has been looking to the wrong gods to solve his problems and to turn the graveyard into a garden again. The application of brainpower and science to his dilemma has not proved to be a panacea for humanity. In *The Unexpected Universe,* Loren Eiseley comments: "But what of the empire of science? Does not its word leap as fast as light, is it not the creator of incalculable wealth, is not space its plaything? Its weapons are monstrous; its eye is capable of peering beyond millions of light years."

Of such "buoyant optimism," Eiseley declares: "science is human; it is of human devising and manufacture. It has not prevented war; it has perfected it. It has not abolished cruelty or corruption; it has enabled these abominations to be practiced on a scale unknown before in human history."

What this noted anthropologist wrote with perception and insight in *The Immense Journey* leads us in the right direction: "The need is not really for more brains, the need now is for a gentler, a more tolerant people than those who won for us against the ice, the tiger, and the bear. The hand that hefted the ax, out of some old blind allegiance to the past fondles the machine gun as lovingly. It is a habit man will have to break to survive, but the roots go very deep."

That's it! A radical solution is called for—something to get down to and kill this "root system"—or mankind, and all life will be doomed. James S. Stewart once said, "Unless the kingdom of evil is intersected at some point from above by the spirit of truth, there is no hope at all." That's what God has done through Christ and the gospel.

God's purpose for man was revealed in the garden—not only to take dominion over the earth and rule it, but to love life, nurture, and preserve it as his precious gift—and he confirmed his intentions for mankind at Golgotha. The cross plunged into the ground at Calvary is the wedge God used to pry open the hardened hearts of men so that they might love each other as Christ loved them.

The gospel is still the answer! Christ can penetrate and change the human heart so that man can love again. Only through him can the graveyard be a garden again!

4.

Genesis 3:3-6:

God said, "You shall not eat of the fruit of the tree which is in the midst of the garden, neither shall you touch it, lest you die." But the serpent said to the woman, "You will not die. For God knows that when you eat of it your eyes will be opened, and you will be like God, knowing good and evil." . . . she took of its fruit and ate; and she also gave some to her husband, and he ate.

The Danger of Being Human

Satan seems to have had a very easy time with man in the garden. It is a simple matter to deceive men when conditions are right. And everything was just perfect for Satan's temptation of man in the Garden of Eden. All conditions were favorable to him. Man was in paradise. He had everything necessary to the sustenance and enrichment of life; he needed nothing more. He was on intimate terms with his maker; his life was full. It must have been like "taking candy from a baby." All Satan had to do was suggest to man that he was immortal and indestructible—as is God—and he would fall. It all went according to plan. Man was deceived . . . and he succumbed to the temptation to try to become God.

There was nothing to it. Success went to Satan's head; at first try he had discovered how to get control of men through deception. Small wonder that he kept to this course; nothing succeeds like success.

When man was expelled from the garden and thrust into the rest of the world, Satan's task became more complicated. He now had to deceive man into thinking he was still in a garden, and that it was man's. Once Satan convinces someone that he is the ruler of his paradise—however tiny it might be—the rest of it is still easy. Man thinks he is "like God," or *is* God, and he plays into Satan's hands. Too late he discovers he is in the devil's den and not in the garden of the gods.

The danger of being human has always been the same—the temptation to think one is not merely "God-like," made in his image, but to think he has the power of God, that he *is* God.

Satan's ultimate test came with Jesus Christ. He used all of his cunning on Christ, trying to get him to change the deserted place where he had been for 40 days into a garden again, attempting to make him think he was totally indestructible, and tempting him to see the whole world as a garden that was really his. But he failed miserably—and right then and there the world was a garden again. Restoration had begun.

With the deception and fall of man, Satan demonstrates time and again his ability to turn the world into a graveyard; with the defeat of Satan when he tempted Jesus Christ, God reiterates his purpose for the world—a garden for mankind to manage and populate—and reassures mankind that he has the power to fulfill his plans. He does not intend that man should totally destroy the world and himself in the process!

It has always seemed to me that Edgar Allen Poe's horror tale, "The Pit and the Pendulum," is a vivid secular interpretation of the power God has to save man from the almost inevitable destruction of the devil and his forces of evil. Poe tells about a man condemned by the Inquisition to a dungeon and death in Toledo, Spain. No escape seems possible.

First, the man, groping his way around the walls of the dungeon in total darkness to discover its dimensions and characteristics, falls and discovers that his head is hanging over an almost bottomless pit, a pit meant to be his grave. He faints and when he awakens he is tied down beneath a swinging pendulum with a curved blade attached to its end; each "swish," as it passes back and forth over him, brings the blade closer to his breast. A more horrible death than the pit is ahead of him. In desperation, as the blade gets near his chest, he finds a way out; he is able to reach a bowl of greasy meat that his captors had placed by one hand to keep him alive during this torture. He rubs the grease and meat on his bonds, and the rats climb up and chew through them, just as he is about to be cut in two. He faints again. For a third time he awakens in the dungeon and smells molten metal; the walls are closing in on him and death is certain, either from the molten metal or the pit. Just as he is about to go over the edge of the pit to his death, a strong hand grabs him and he is pulled back to safety. It was the hand of General LaSalle, leader of the French forces that have put down the Inquisition and saved him. The man went from a graveyard to a garden in that instant.

God has the power to save man, 20th century man whose time is running out, but his deliverance won't come about automatically and unexpectedly as Poe might have been picturing it in his story. Rather, God's power must be appreciated and appropriated by man today as it was by Christ in his temptation and throughout his whole life.

Paul saw the secret and passed it on to the Philippians:

> Have this mind among yourselves, which you have in Christ Jesus, who, though he was in the form of God, did not count equality with God a thing to be grasped, but emptied himself, taking the form of a servant, being born in the likeness of men. And being found in human form he humbled himself and became obedient unto death, even death on a cross. Therefore God has highly exalted him . . .

God will save mankind, but men must hear his Word, know that he alone is God the Creator and Father, and obey his commands while trusting in his plans for the garden.

Some time ago an unusual "special" was shown on television in Great Britain. It had to do with the life of Mary Slessor, the young Scottish girl known vaguely to most informed church people as a kind of female David Livingstone. She spent most of her life as a missionary in that part of Africa now known as Nigeria. Her credo, so simple yet so profound, came to be widely known: "I love him and I trust him." Nothing could dull her sense of wonder and awe for God and his world. One of the last entries in her diary read, "I received such a lovely pair of spectacles for Christmas." When she died in Africa, it is said that a mournful chant was passed from village to village where she had ministered and witnessed to her faith in God, "Our mother is dead. Our mother is dead." They erected a memorial to her, and, according to an African student, they have not forgotten her. The God of the garden—who watered and tended her spirit—became evident to the Africans in everything she did and said. In her and for her, God was really God.

If the danger in being human is to be deceived into thinking one is like God, the secret to being human is to know that God is God and that men are his creatures and servants on earth. Only of God can we sing, "Immortal, invisible, God only wise." And once we are informed and enlightened by the gospel of Christ, who put down Satan with, "Man shall not live by bread alone, but by every word that proceeds out of the mouth of God," who turned his back on the evil one with "You shall not tempt the Lord your God," and who glorified God and changed graveyard into garden right then with "You shall worship the Lord your God and him only shall you serve," we are able to sing a hymn of trust and hope:

> I know no life divided,
> O Lord of life, from thee;

In thee is life provided
For all mankind and me;
I know no death, O Jesus,
Because I live in thee;
Thy death it is which frees us
From death eternally.
(SBH 573, stanza 2)

When mankind knows that God is God, through the gospel of our Lord, the earth will be a garden again.

5.

Genesis 6:6-7:

And the Lord was sorry that he had made man on the earth, and it grieved him to his heart. So the Lord said, "I will blot out man whom I have created from the face of the ground . . . for I am sorry that I have made them."

Genesis 7:17-23, esp. 23:

He blotted out every living thing that was upon the face of the ground, man and animals and creeping things and birds of the air; they were blotted out from the earth. Only Noah was left . . .

Survival or
Extinction?

The exciting and near tragic flight to the moon of
Apollo 13 in April, 1970, temporarily united most of
the people on earth. For the space of several days, na-
tional rivalries and political animosities were forgotten;
the astronauts, Jim Lovell, Fred Haise, and John
Swigert, were simply human beings. They belonged
to every nation and every people on earth after the
explosion disabled their spaceship almost a quarter of
a million miles from the earth.

The flight of Apollo 13 was altered abruptly from
an adventurous journey to the moon, begun in the
hope of bringing back rocks to a rescue mission. The
mission's intention was clearly revealed in its slogan,
Ex Luna, Scientia—From the Moon, Knowledge. In
the hours after the explosion it became apparent that
the trip had become a flight for survival; a near miracle
seemed necessary to get the astronauts and their command module back home safely. The moon landing

was abandoned and attention centered on the critical calculations and maneuvers that were the imperatives of the moment.

According to the first reports, shocked people began to pray for the astronauts. Special religious services were held around the world. Friend and foe alike expressed concern and offered cooperation and whatever aid they could to help with the rescue operations. The whole experience was unique in the history of mankind; never before had there been such a concerted effort to affect the rescue of just three persons. Apollo 13 turned into a much more significant and successful journey than was anticipated, and the climax of it all was the "splashdown" in the Pacific and the brief prayer of thanksgiving offered by a Navy chaplain on the deck of the rescue ship.

In retrospect, the command module, the *Odyssey,* and the lunar module, the *Aquarius,* might have carried a single and older name, the *Ark.* Thousands of years ago there was a water mission for the survival of life on the earth. And suddenly Apollo 13 became symbolic of that ancient ark and man's predicament on earth. Some people began to compare the problems of survival in space with survival on earth; the same set of difficulties besets man on "Spaceship Earth" as on Apollo 13—oxygen to breathe, pure water to drink, an adequate food supply, disposal of waste, sufficient space, constant "people-pressure," plus the tension resulting from the uncertainties of success. The ark must have had them, too, plus a population explosion. That precarious trip took a year and ten days!

It might have been simply that people around the world had their imaginations excited and their sympathy stimulated by the combination of competence, bravery, and "cool" that the astronauts displayed. But it was more than that; men throughout the world suddenly became aware of the predicament at hand, the possible extinction of all life. Earth needs a gigantic rescue operation. Some say that the end of the earth is at hand, that there is no future.

Isn't it amazing? Men have always scoffed and laughed at the "prophets of doom," but nobody laughs today. The signs are too evident; extinction seems to have caught up with humanity and accompanying forms of life as it always has in the past. Nature is relentless in its drive to eradicate inadequate forms of life and to move to higher forms. "In fact," writes John H. Ostrom, "The fossil record shows that extinction is the ultimate fate of all species. Of the millions of species of animals and plants that have lived during the billion or so years since life began, most—probably more than 90%—are extinct."

And man is next!

Too many circumstances seem to have combined into a cataclysmic crisis that seems impossible of solution. The old problems are still with the human race—the bomb for example—and may constitute greater threats than ever before. Scientists say that the possibility of atomic war increases every year; by 2000 A.D. the chances of an atomic-hydrogen holocaust will be one in two—50%.

Before the trees and shrubs grew large in the area where I live, I could see a home with a bomb shelter built in the back yard. I can't see the house or the yard now, but the bomb shelter is still there. Nobody laughs any more. Nor do they scoff at the man who bought an older home and proceeded to renovate it from top to bottom. In addition, he built a spacious and comfortable family room, and under it, a reinforced concrete bomb shelter. These signs of the times are pertinent—and indicative of a struggle for survival.

But what good would be served if some could survive atomic warfare only to discover that the world is uninhabitable? Man can't live in a graveyard!

And should the earth be spared extinction by the bomb, the other problems that threaten all life, and whose effects on life and environment are scientifically predictable, becloud the future of life on earth. Overpopulation, pollution, famine, strife, crime, corruption, and neglect will be so marked before the end of the 20th century as to make extinction inevitable. One scientist has pointed beyond the evident problems to unseen and, as yet, unpredictable threats to all life: "It may already be too late to save the seas. Right now they could be poisoned beyond reclamation." If so, all life is doomed. There is no hope.

A few brave souls dare to be optimistic, and they

speak of a possible future for man and the earth. Joseph Platt in the foreword to William Pollard's *Man on a Spaceship* insists, "No one can foretell the future. Even the most imaginative and farsighted men of the mid-19th century—men like Jules Verne in technology and Admiral Mahan in naval strategy—saw only in dim outline a few features of the middle of the 20th century. . . . We do have some limited success in foretelling the future (through the scientific method). . . ." More importantly he continues, "There is another way of dealing with the future, which is to assume—to take it on faith—that there is a purpose in human life and that enough of this purpose is available to us through the religious insights we inherit or can learn to enable us to choose between the uncertainties of the present with trust in the future." Apollo 13 and the ark, as well, were ventures in that kind of faith.

God made it clear long, long ago that he does not intend to exterminate all life on the earth, including those called mankind; Noah and seven other humans survived the flood that covered the earth. And because he had a purpose for man and the earth, he provided an escape route. A man of faith took it—and he and his survived the experience of a watery grave to find themselves in a garden again.

Lent has to be a time when we all realize that we are getting what we deserve because of our sin, but it must equally be a season when the purposes of God for man and all life—deliverance, reconciliation, restoration, and hope—are reiterated. Only when we hear the Lord saying again, "Behold, we are going up to Jerusalem, and everything that is written of the Son of man by the prophets will be accomplished. For he will be delivered to the Gentiles, and will be mocked and shamefully treated and spit upon; they will scourge him and kill him, and on the third day he will rise." And Luke adds, "But they understood none of these things. . ." (Luke 18:31-34).

Strangely enough, we may not have seen all the implications of Jesus' journey through actual death to survival for the future and destiny of man. But this much is clear: through faith in our dead and risen Lord, we are freed from our fear of death and extinction, strengthened to endure the sufferings of the struggle for survival, and given the power of his resurrection that we may have high hopes for the future through that love that passes all knowledge.

Hope in the future will not come cheaply for us, even though we call ourselves Christian. We must go through the waters of a kind of death to enter the earth again—graveyard to garden. The sign and directive are in the cross of Christ. Could it be that the ark and Apollo 13 show us the way? Were both not washed by the sea before their inhabitant-survivors reached dry land—the garden, earth—again?

For us there is the font—and death—and life.

The garden, not the graveyard, is God's purpose for man and our destiny in Christ.

6.

Genesis 6:22:
Noah did this; he did all that God com-
manded him.

One Secret
for Survival

Survival in this world and the continued existence of life on earth depends on man's obedience to God's Word more than on the ingenuity of science.

That's the way it was in the time of the Flood. The obedience of *one man,* according to the Bible, was the secret to the survival of the species of life, including man, who lived on the earth at that time. Noah heard God's commandments concerning the construction of the ark; he took them seriously and diligently did his best to follow the directions he was given.

The simple survival of life today, let alone the restoration of the earth to some semblance of the paradise God made it in the beginning, will require the obedience of everyone. Vision and effort on the part of a few people will not be sufficient. A concerted drive to clean up the earth, eliminate pollution, banish war, poverty, and suffering is required. Nobody is exempt.

Therefore the kingdom of God in this age is like

two men who belonged to a suburban congregation. They lived in a garden-like atmosphere. Both attended the worship services of their church with regularity. They were fortunate enough to attend worship in a place where the Word of God was understood and preached effectively by dedicated pastors. The two men were representative of most of the members of the congregation, the residents of that community, and a majority of people who called themselves "the people of God."

One man was a middle-aged executive, employed by one of the largest corporations in the world. He was competent and talented with the necessary ability to survive in the business world. His salary and responsibilities were commensurate with his position. He merited respect from colleagues, church members, and the people of his community. He worked hard; he kept his home in good condition; he obeyed the letter of the law. He was a good citizen and, in obvious respects, a worthy member of the Christian church.

This man was asked to participate in various programs of social action and fellowship in his congregation. He always refused, saying, "I go to church on Sunday. I give regularly. And that's all I have time for." He was usually apologetic about his refusal and offered excuses: "When I'm not working, I just have to relax. I find my social contacts and relaxation on the golf course. I have so much pressure on me that I have to get away as often as possible, so my wife and I take golfing vacations when we can—to Arizona, the Bahamas, or Scotland. Nobody can reach me there, and I get rid of my tensions and problems."

Finally, he was asked by a team from the church to take part financially in a building fund drive for the erection of a parish house and community center. Both were desperately needed for work with young people in the community. "I don't have any children in this congregation. I can't see how this affects me." Pressed farther, he blustered, "I don't believe in church building programs," and firmly, "I won't tie myself down with a pledge."

It was obvious to the visitors that he was both irritated and defensive; they stood up to leave. Then the man, the regular churchgoer, who had the ability to give physically and financially to the work of the kingdom, dropped a bombshell: "I can't give because my objective at present is to complete a financial retirement program I have set up. Nothing is going to keep me from finishing it!"

A poem flashed through the mind of one of the visitors:

> I lived for myself, I thought for myself,
> For myself and none other beside;
> As if Jesus had never lived,
> As if he had never died.

After thanking the man and his wife, who finally joined him and supported his position, the visitors left.

They realized as they went to make their next call

that the man was not unique. One of the visitors taught
Sunday school and he remembered occasions when he
and his students had discussed the nature of the Christian life. Most agreed about the ways in which Chris-
tians should recognize responsibilities and fulfill them.
But when they planned projects, only a few would
participate. The others would say, "We went up to the
lake," or, "We got a new snowmobile, and we had to
go and try it out," or, "I was so busy I just forgot about
it."

> I lived for myself, I thought for myself,
> For myself and none other . . .

The man's story, the visitors knew, was a common
story often told in their church and throughout the
whole church—with all sorts of variations. And they
knew, too, that they had come face to face with the
real form of "heart disease"—self-service and pride—
at the center of most of the problems that threaten to
wipe out the last vestiges of the garden and turn earth
into a graveyard through the extermination of life.

The other man was young—still in college—but he
had vision in addition to intelligence, leadership ability, social concern, and the drive to do something for
man and his earth. He had a career goal in life—to
become a lawyer—and he worked toward that goal.
But he was convinced that as a human being and
a Christian he had other responsibilities which wouldn't
wait until his personal objectives were realized. You
might say he had a call from God, a clear-cut directive

to serve God and man. He set out to answer that call, not merely in a building fund drive, but in more dramatic ways.

He organized the young people in his school, then in schools throughout his state, for various service projects. The culmination of his dream and efforts came in the famous "Handshoe Hollow" project to the people of an isolated and poverty-ridden section of Appalachia. In the summer of 1969, some 115 young people passed up summer jobs that might have paid well—sacrificing cars, clothing, albums, and dates— to go to Handshoe Hollow as volunteer workers for six weeks. They had raised over $17,000 to finance the project, and had collected a truck load of clothing which they took with them and distributed to the people who needed them. They did all kinds of tasks —built community centers, helped with child care and housekeeping—they even built a road so that the children of that community could get out to school in the winter. It was no "lark," but they intend to go back again—and to other places as well.

It all happened because one young man was reared in the faith of our fathers—not simply because he happened to be endowed with extraordinary ability and talent. The Word he heard was responsible for the vision and the motivation to do something for others. Had he been primarily concerned about himself, he might have accelerated his college course, finished sooner, and gone into the practice of law or politics at a much earlier age. Had he wished, he could have been earning money for himself and guaranteeing his future financially and in other ways. But he heard the cries of suffering and dying humanity, the hurt and the hungry, and attempted to respond as a child of God.

Two men heard the same preacher, in the same place, and in similar conditions. But one heard some words being spoken to human beings; the other heard the Word of God . . . and he did it, kept it, with imagination and persistence, with self-lessness and zeal.

And there was, and is, another one who knew and taught the kingdom and God's secrets. It is by giving oneself unselfishly, without reservation that the earth can be preserved and that mankind can survive.

Such is the secret of survival in this graveyard—earth—which God wants for a garden.

7.

Genesis 8:20-21:

Then Noah built an altar to the Lord, and took of every clean animal and of every clean bird, and offered burnt offerings on the altar. And when the Lord smelled the pleasing odor, the Lord said in his heart, "I will never again curse the ground because of man, for the imagination of man's heart is evil from his youth; neither will I ever again destroy every living creature as I have done."

Genesis 9:9-13:

"Behold, I establish my covenant with you and your descendants after you . . . that never again shall all flesh be cut off by the waters of a flood. . . . This is the sign of the covenant which I make between me and you and every living creature that is with you, for all future generations: I set my bow in the cloud, and it shall be a sign of the covenant between me and the earth."

John 19:17:

So they took Jesus, and he went out, bearing his own cross, to the place called the place of a skull, which is called in Hebrew Golgotha.

The Cross Holds
Up the Rainbow
(Good Friday)

The earth, God's garden, has been a graveyard twice in the history of man, according to the Bible. Today we live in the fear that it may soon be a graveyard for a third time—and forever!

When Noah survived the Flood, spending over a year cooped up in that ark, he set foot into a graveyard, for no forms of life survived on land with the exception of the creatures on that ship. The bones of the corpses claimed by the Flood had been covered up by the shifting sands and soil. The earth was washed clean; it was a garden again, much like the beginning of creation. An eerie silence must have greeted the first beings to disembark from that boat; only the sounds of the animals who still lived could be heard. Echoes were everywhere. But Noah built an altar, offered sacrifices of thanksgiving to God, and got an answer: "I will never again curse the ground with a flood. . . I establish my covenant between you and your descendants after you. . . I set my bow in the cloud, and it shall be a sign of the covenant."

The earth was a garden again. Men thought it would be a garden forever, regardless of what they might do.

But the earth became a graveyard again, this time symbolically, when men outwardly revealed their sin by crucifying Jesus Christ on a hill outside Jerusalem, Golgotha—the place of a skull. When Jesus died there, all were sentenced again, "to dust you shall return." For a time on that day we know as Good Friday, the earth was the graveyard of man in the place of the skull.

The skull was man's, the cross was Christ's, and the combination spelled *life,* not *death,* for all mankind! In that place of execution and extinction, God himself set up the cross as a sign of his undying love for the sinful sons of Noah with whom he had made that eternal covenant. God had been wronged again by the men he made to be creatures, who "in the imagination of their hearts" thought themselves to be God. The cross and skull spell out forgiveness and reconciliation, restoration and hope. The cross holds up the rainbow.

"Cross-like" acts occur every now and then and set our hearts to singing in this self-destroying world. A man was driving home one afternoon, and as he turned the corner of the street on which he lived, he saw a young girl taking a picture of her father. Usually there is nothing special about such a phenomenon, but this was something different. This had been a broken home; the father had deserted his wife and three teen-age children. He had been gone for months. And then one night their telephone rang, and husband and father said, "May I come home?" He was welcomed with open arms; they were a family again. The young girl taking the picture was the youngest child, and she may have been the one most deeply hurt by her father's act. Right there on their doorstep, out where everyone could see them, the girl was announcing to the world that all was well. Something profound had taken place through an act of love and forgiveness—and the future, that had been as unyielding as a tomb, was wide open for them now.

That cross said, and will say forever, "God was in Christ reconciling the world to himself." God still gives life—and a garden—even in the place of a death-skull. The cross announces, "I will still keep my covenant with man!" And he has. The cross holds up the rain-bow.

Man is the covenant-breaker, not God! God was not merely gracious and loving in the beginning, he is continually faithful to himself and his creatures. He cannot be otherwise. He is God and he is good. But man is something else! How can you trust a God who can't be seen, who supposedly speaks but can't be heard with ears, who "opens his hand and blesses every living thing" but the hand can't be touched, let alone grasped and clung to?

The cross of Christ gives open testimony to the fact

that one man was willing to be a man, even though he was the Son of God. He took God at his word. He communed with him in prayer. He served God, not self as other men do. He had to be eliminated simply because he was what a man ought to be, a creature of faith and selfless service to God. The world can't tolerate people who live consciously as children of God! The cross for them!

Could Rudyard Kipling have been thinking of a skull, a cross, and a sign above that cross, "This is the king of the Jews," when he wrote his short story, "The Man Who Would Be King"? Did he have his tongue in his cheek as he told his yarn about two men, Dan Dravot and Peachey Carnahan, who invaded a remote and isolated make-believe country, Kafiristan, and were welcomed as gods by the people who had never seen white men or modern weapons and other trappings of the civilized world? They made them their kings, as well as their gods. And all went well until Dan, the chief king, decided that he needed a wife. When he chose one from the women, the people turned on their god-kings; they pushed Dan over a cliff and crucified Peachey in the winter snow—simply because "gods don't take wives." Their "gods" were rejected because they were too much like men; Christ died partly because he was too much like God! The cross that holds up the rainbow calls men to repentance!

The cross says that Christ was willing to turn a grave-yard into a garden again; he came to earth to do just that. His body, the church, offers evidence to the world that God is alive, cares, still has a "garden plan" for humanity—and has the power to accomplish these things. And his children, people of faith, who are drawn to the cross "in the place of a skull," affirm by word and sacrificial deeds that the man on the cross is truly King of Kings and Lord of Lords!

The message of the cross to this age, when the earth seems about to be a graveyard for the third and final time, is clearly this: "to live with him, we must be willing to die with him." Noah and his loved ones did this; rode out a long, dark, and stormy night of death in the ark—and landed in a garden again. Again and again, men have dared to trust God even in the face of death. The only glorious thing about war is that some men will sacrifice themselves so that others might survive and be reunited with their loved ones at home. The irony of acts like these is that they ought to be done in the ordinary times of life, not when men are trying to destroy themselves and their world by overt acts of aggression. The road to the garden still passes through the graveyard. It always will! His cross holds up the rainbow of promise and hope.

The cross in the skull is our hope today. Christ is Lord of life and death. Through his own life and death, he changed the graveyard into a garden. He draws us to himself and his cross so that he might do it again!

Jesus, may our hearts be burning
  With more fervent love for thee;
May our eyes be ever turning
  To thy Cross of agony;
Till in glory, parted never
  From the blessed Saviour's side,
Graven in our hearts forever,
  Dwell the Cross, the Crucified.

(SBH 69, stanza 3)

The cross holds up the rainbow!

8.

Luke 24:1-7:

But on the first day of the week, at early dawn, they went to the tomb. . . . And they found the stone rolled away from the tomb, but when they went in they did not find the body. While they were perplexed about this, behold, two men stood by them in dazzling apparel; and as they were frightened and bowed their faces to the ground, the men said to them, "Why do you seek the living among the dead? Remember how he told you, while he was still in Galilee, that the Son of man must be delivered into the hands of sinful men, and be crucified, and on the third day rise."

The Candle That Lights Up the Garden

(Easter Vigil)

One candle burns more brightly than all the others.
    It is the light that ushers in the dawn of Easter,
        the Christ Candle, announcing the glorious news,
"He is risen! He is not here. Come see the place where
he lay!"
The executioner's hammer, as he drove the nails
through Jesus' flesh
    Made the sparks fly as it struck those spikes.
They thought they were smothering another spark,
    his life—
        when iron met iron
        and met resistance only in the wood of the Tree.
They were trying to put out that Light that had come
into the world
        and illumined another Judean night
            with its brightness.

Witnesses said it was as if
  "The glory of the Lord shone upon them,"
    the Light was so bright.
and a Star shone in the sky that night,
  burning more brightly than the other stars,
  beckoning men to follow its rays
  and see the Christ Child,
  born in Bethlehem,
    the Light of the world.

The Light was too bright for men.
It hurt their eyes
  and burned right down into their hearts.
It made their hearts burn, too.
  They couldn't stand the pain.

So they put out the Light
  by pinning him to a tree
  forever to be a butterfly on display
    to serve as a warning
    to those who sought out the Light
    and the meaning of Life.
They let his blood drip on the ground,
  as oil seeps out of a cracked lamp,
    until it is all gone,
      and can burn no more.
When the last drop fell to the earth,
  they knew that the Light would go out
    forever.

And the light did go out.

But as it did, God was there,
  catching that last spark of life,
  cupping his hands about it,
  protecting—fanning it all the time
    so that it would burst into flame again
      at the appointed time—
      the third day.

It was almost as if the sparks that flew from hammer
and nails
  had fallen on a long fuse
  connected to an explosive charge—
    the secret of life.

No one heard a sputtering sound in the stillness of
that night,
  but the fuse was smoldering
    all during that blackest of nights,
      through another dark day—more like night than
      day for the faithful—
      and through another darker, even more unendur-
      able, night of doubt and despair.

The spark made its way to the end of the fuse
  in the darkness before the dawn
    of the third day
      and light burst forth in the tomb,

piercing the black veil of death,
lighting up the world again:

"Behold the stone is rolled away,
    And shining ones have come to say,
        'He is not here, but is risen!'
    The night of death is past and gone,
    Arise and greet the glorious morn,
        'He is not here, but is risen!' "

The Light they extinguished burns again—
    more brightly than before!

It shone into the darkness of Golgotha,
    burned out of the empty eye sockets of a Skull,
    so that men might see the power of God
        that can make a graveyard a garden again.

It seemed like the brightness of the sun itself,
    for death was defeated on that radiant morn,
    just as sin had met its match three days before;
        He is yet—and forever—
            the Light of the world,
        giving life to the dead
        and hope to the hopeless people of this world.

A church, built at the confluence of two great high-
ways, in a distant land, expresses this Easter message in
a unique way:

A crucifix holds Christ's body over one of the altars.
Christ is dead.
The spark of life has long since gone out of him.
But the crown of thorns they had placed on his head
was alive.
The thorns grew like a vine
  down his body and the cross
    to the ground
      where the two growing ends, like tendrils,
        grew out over the ground as though they were
        trying to cover the whole earth.
At some signal from God, a signal unheard by men,
  the growing ends of the thorn-vine
  turned heaven-ward.
    They reached for the sun
      and caught its radiant beams
      in the candles their curled fingers held.
  The light of Easter burns in that place
    and shines into all the world!

One candle burns more brightly than all the rest!
    The light still gives life.
  The graveyard becomes a garden again
    through the power of the God who controls
    all things,
      and loves the creatures
      to whom he has given Life.

One candle—that wondrous light of Easter and the
risen Lord—burns more brightly than all the others:

"Gratefully our hearts adore Him,
As his light once more appears;
Bowing down in joy before Him;
Rising up from griefs and tears.

Christ is risen! Alleluia!
Risen our victorious Head!
Sing his praises! Alleluia!
Christ is risen from the Dead!"

One candle burns more brightly than the others
and it will burn forever
in the garden God has given to man.

9.

John 20:11-16:

But Mary stood weeping outside the tomb, and as she wept she stooped to look into the tomb; and she saw two angels in white, sitting where the body of Jesus had lain, one at the head and one at the feet. They said to her, "Woman, why are you weeping?" She said to them, "Because they have taken away my Lord, and I do not know where they have laid him." Saying this, she turned around and saw Jesus standing, but she did not know it was Jesus. Jesus said to her, "Woman, why are you weeping? Whom do you seek?" Supposing him to be the gardener, she said to him, "Sir, if you have carried him away, tell me where you have laid him, and I will take him away." Jesus said to her, "Mary." She turned and said to him in Hebrew, "Rabboni!" (which means Teacher).

A Graveyard
Becomes a Garden
(Easter)

Mary was right in the first place. It really was the gardener she saw in the garden on that day we now call Easter. God brought Christ forth from the grave into the garden to renew and tend the life of God's creatures as the living Lord.

Scholars and biblical archaeologists say it all happened in that spot, now within the walls of the "old city" of Jerusalem—the city of peace—and they are probably right. Almost everything changes in two thousand years. The city is not the same. The walls are in a different location—parts of them, at least. And the place of the tomb has changed. Man, it is said, cut away the walls of the grave in time and built a church over the place where Jesus had lain. The Church of the Holy Sepulchre is an invitation to all men "to come see the place where he lay." The place barely excites the imagination, except, perhaps, at the Orthodox portion of the shrine that permits one a view of the grave slab itself. There, with Mary, the pilgrim must stoop to look into what is said to have been Jesus' grave.

His real grave—for the world had to be able to see for itself that Christ had really died—was the place of the Skull. That's why "Gordon's Calvary" is much more stimulating and sentimentally satisfying; it approximates the biblical description of the Skull and the cave. The cross is easily visible in the mind's eye on top of that little hill where another graveyard now exists. And on the cliff side, the Skull is clearly seen, with empty cave-like eye sockets and, below them, the entrance to the tomb—an open mouth of a larger grave, the earth, that seeks to swallow up the life that it thinks *it* has given to men. Abutting the Skull-graveyard is a lovely little garden, set in the midst of old buildings, alley-like streets, and the debris of mankind that has accumulated outside the city walls. A graveyard has become a garden again!

Jesus lives! He is Lord of the garden, earth, and he nurtures all life in the garden God has made. In a chapter, "Prisoner of the Sand," from his *Wind, Sand and Stars,* Antoine de Saint-Exupéry unintentionally illuminates the relevance and meaning of Easter for humanity. He does this by retelling the story of an ill-fated flight from Paris to Saigon begun late in 1935. A series of misfortunes resulted in a plane crash in the Libyan desert of North Africa. Antoine and his mechanic, Prévot, miraculously survived the crash.

The two men made some reckonings, when daylight came to the desert, and determined that they were far off the caravan routes. They must leave the plane and attempt to get to a place where they might be rescued. With very little water and virtually no food, they started out. For five days they kept walking, using their ingenuity and fortitude to keep themselves alive in the scorching heat of the day and the bitter cold of the night. On the fifth day, they realized that hope had run out—death was near. They had been fooled again and again by mirages—men, animals, oases, even a lake. Their throats were dry, their gullets hard, the voices raspy. "The end is near." But just then something, instinct, perhaps, gave them new hope.

Antoine writes: "I swear to you that something is about to happen. I swear that life has sprung in this desert. I swear that this emptiness, this stillness, has suddenly become more stirring than a tumult in a public square." A graveyard was about to become a garden.

He continues: "Prévot! Footprints! We are saved!"

"We had wandered from the trail of the human species; we had cast ourselves forth from the tribe; we had found ourselves alone on earth and forgotten by the universal migration; and here, imprinted in the sand, were the divine and naked feet of man!"

"Look, Prévot, here two men stood together and then separated."

"Here a camel knelt."

"Here . . ."

"But it was not true that we were already saved. It was not enough to squat down and wait. Before long we should be past saving. . . ."

"We went on. Suddenly I heard a cock crow. . . ." They both saw a Bedouin on a camel, shouted, but couldn't be heard; he rode out of sight.

"We saw in profile on the dune another Arab. We shouted, but our shouts were whispers. . . . Still the Bedouin stared with averted face away from us."

"At last, slowly, slowly he began a right angle turn in our direction. At the very second when he came face to face with us, I thought, the curtain would come down. At the very second when his eyes met ours, thirst would vanish and by this man would death and the mirages be wiped out. Let this man but make a quarter-turn left and the world is changed. Let him but bring his torso round, but sweep the scene with a glance, and like a god he can create life."

"The miracle had come to pass. He was walking towards us over the sand like a god over the waves." He brought water, refuge, restoration—life.

Time is running out on the human race. The earth is like a deserted place where men cannot survive without divine help. And we of the 20th century know better than any other people who ever lived that we have gotten ourselves into this predicament by the things we have done in God's garden. We even know the ways—pollution, war, persecution, greed, population explosion—that we have turned the garden into a graveyard. We cry out for help, but no one seems to hear or help.

Easter finds a man walking toward us from a grave. He turns the earth into a garden again as he approaches. He is the one men have been searching for in their desperation. Suddenly we realize that this man in our graveyard has been looking for us all the time, so that he might help us: "I am the good shepherd . . . . I come to save the lost . . . . I lay down my life for the sheep."

On Easter we ought to remember a hymn we have sung before:

> I sought the Lord and afterward I knew
>   He moved my soul to seek Him, seeking me.
> It was not I that found, O Saviour true;
>   No, I was found of thee!
>
> *(SBH 473, stanza 1)*

Golgotha is the sure sign of his seeking us out. The empty grave in the garden tells us he is alive, still searching for all of us on earth. He is offering life to mankind so that the earth, which more and more resembles a graveyard, might become a garden once again.

In her grief Mary mistakenly thought Jesus to be the gardener at dawn of that Easter day. If our eyes have been opened in our desperation so that we know our prospects on earth are only death and extinction, we discover that she was right in her first assumption.

Jesus is the gardener—God has placed the earth and man in his hands—and he tends the garden well.

Once and for all God has changed the graveyard into a garden—and the living Lord of the garden will keep it that way!